Islam 101

A Beginners Guide to Understanding the Muslim Faith

A SHORT BOOK PROJECT

FIRST EDITION

AUGUST 19, 2019

Contents

List of Figures

Preface

While many online resources are available to understand the basics of Islam and learn about Muslims, the information is scattered and often not an authentic representation of the religion. Sometimes it may be too detailed for a beginner who wants a concise overview of the basics. This book is an effort to describe the basics of Islam in an easy-to-read format.

This is not a theological reference and should not be taken as such. Vast amounts of scholarly material is available in the form of many books for an in-depth study of Islam. Anyone can start with reading the Quran, which is the primary source about Islam. While the Quran is in Arabic language, many translation are available in almost all major languages. However, keep in mind that any translation represents the translator's understanding of the Quran and is not the actual book itself.

Free copies of Quran are also available from a number of organizations. Please see Appendix A for a list of resources where you can read Quran online or get a free printed copy.

Book Audience: Who Should Read It?

People who want to get a basic understanding of Islam and Muslims will find this book as a useful resource. For example:

- School teachers who need to better understand their Muslim students

- Non-Muslims brothers and sisters in humanity who have an interest in Islam and want to learn the basics

- Participants of Islam 101 and interfaith events arranged by different communities across the globe

- New Muslims who are just starting to learn the basics of Islam

- Young Muslim students who have just started learning their religion

Effort has been made to keep this simple and brief. For details on a specific topic, please contact a reputed scholar who has a good understanding of the Quran and the Islamic Traditions.

Book Organization

The book is organized into small chapters. Each chapter covers a specific topic. The main objective is to keep it simple and short with a minimalistic approach. Instead of long paragraphs, you will find list-items in many places to present important points.

> *Text with a vertical bar on the left-hand side (like this one) is a translation of some part of Quran with chapter and verse numbers marked.*

Initial chapters are focused on fundamental articles of faith and beliefs while the latter ones provide a short summary about Muslims.

Getting the Latest Copy of Book, Reproduction and Customization

You can get the latest version of this book from online book stores as well as download a free PDF version. You are free to print copies of this book and distribute as you like. However, if you want to add a name and a short introduction to your organization to your copy for distribution, please contact us via email 4shortbook@gmail.com with the following information:

- Name of your organization

- Contact information (Contact Person, Phone, Email)

- A one-paragraph introduction of your organization

- A high-resolution version of your logo, if you want to print it with your organization name

Once this information is received, you will get a modified version of this book in PDF format.

Your Feedback

Your feedback to improve this text is very important. You can send your feedback via email to 4shortbook@gmail.com .

Acknowledgments

We used LATEXtypesetting system for a print-quality version of this text. For this, the author is thankful to the creators and contributors to LATEXand the open source software movement.

We are also thankful to many people who provided suggestions and feedback to make this book better. This project will not be completed without their feedback and suggestions for improvement.

A Short Book Project Team
August 2019

بِسْمِ اللهِ الرَّحْمَنِ الرَّحِيمِ
In the name of Allah, the most
Beneficent, the most Merciful

The first verse of Quran

1

An Introduction to Islam and Muslims

Islam is the religion of more than one billion Muslims living across the globe. From far eastern Asia to western Africa to the Americas, they come from all countries, many cultural backgrounds, ethnic groups, and speak numerous languages. All of them read the same book, the Holy Quran, and have the same fundamental beliefs. This book is a short introduction to who Muslims are, what they believe in, and pillars on which the building of Islam is based.

The literal translations of word *Islam* are close to *submission* and *peace*. The standard Muslim greeting contains similar word *As Salam Alaikum* which means "peace be upon you".

1.1 Is Islam a New Religion?

Islam is not a new or different religion. Muslims believe that Islam has been the religion of all prophets since the beginning, starting with Adam and Eve. All great prophets including Noah, Abraham, Ismael, Issac, Jacob, Moses, Jesus and others followed the same religion till Prophet Muhammed, Peace Be Upon Him (PBUH), the last messenger to humankind. The Quran makes this point at multiple places. For example, the Quran states to the followers of Abrahamic faiths that Abraham (or *Ibraheem* in Arabic) was not a Christian or a Jew but someone who followed the path of submission to God.

1

1.2   Who are Muslims?

Muslims are the people who follow Islam and submit to God. They believe in the oneness of God and believe Muhammed (PBUH) is the last messenger and Quran is the last book of guidance from God to humankind.

As of 2015, there are more than 1.8 billion Muslims spread across the world. The five countries with the largest Muslim population are Indonesia, Pakistan, India, Bangladesh and Nigeria. The percentage of Muslim in different countries is shown in Figure 1.1[15].

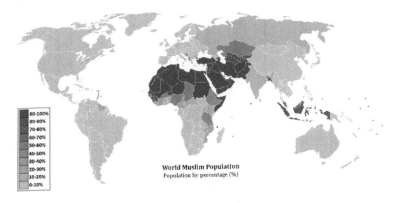

Figure 1.1: World Muslim population by country (Source: Wikipedia)

1.3   What is The Quran?

The Quran is the literal verbatim word of God (Allah) revealed to Prophet Muhammed (PBUH) in Arabic language through angel Gabriel over a period of approximately 23 years. The literal meaning of the word "Quran" is a book that is recited, over and over. It is derived from a *root* Arabic word that most closely translates to "recite" in the English language.

Translations of the Quran are available in many languages including English, although all Muslims refer to the original Arabic text. Any translation is not a replacement of the Arabic text and is considered only the translator's understanding of the Quran.

1.4   How One Becomes a Muslim?

Islam is a very decentralized religion and connects a person directly with his creator without any intermediaries. Becoming a Muslim does not require any special approval from anybody or any specific ritual. Anybody who *says* and *believes* in the following words becomes a Muslim. In some literature it is also known as *Testimony of Faith or Shahadah*.

"I bear witness that there is no deity worth of worship except Allah and that Muhammed is his servant and messenger"

That's it, nothing more, nothing less! Just like there is no approval required to become a Muslim, once a person becomes a Muslim, nobody can and has any authority to expel or excommunicate anyone from Islam.

1.5   What is the Meaning of Allah?

Allah is Arabic word for one and the only God, the Creator and Sustainer of this universe. Allah is not the name of a "Muslim God" as people of other religions in the Middle East, including Christianity, who speak Arabic use this same word for their creator. Bible published in Arabic also uses word Allah to describe God. Figure 1.2 shows the word "Allah' written in Arabic text [8].

Figure 1.2: Word "Allah" written in Arabic

The best description of Allah in the words of Quran is as follows:

> *Say (O Muhammed), He is Allah, the One and Unique, the Self-Sufficient to whom eventually all take their needs. He begets not, nor was He begotten. And none is comparable to Him. - Quran - 112*

And in another place in Quran:

> *He is Allah, the Creator, the Inventor of all things, the Bestower of forms. To Him belong the Best Names. All that is in the heavens and the earth glorify Him. And He is the All-Mighty, the All-Wise. - Quran - 59:24*

There are many other beautiful names used for Allah in Quran commonly known as *Ninety Nine names of Allah.*

> *The most beautiful names belong to Allah, so call on Him by them.* - Quran - 7:180
>
> *He is Allah, other than whom there is no deity, the Sovereign, the Pure, the Perfection, the Bestower of Faith, the Overseer, the Exalted in Might, the Compeller, the Superior. Exalted is Allah above whatever they associate with Him.*
>
> *He is Allah, the Creator, the Inventor, the Fashioner; to Him belong the best names. Whatever is in the heavens and earth is exalting Him. And He is the Exalted in Might, the Wise.*
>
> Quran - 59:23-24

1.6   Islamic Culture and Diversity

Muslims belong to a very pluralistic society of one religion and many cultures. While the core beliefs and practices of all Muslims are the same irrespective where they live, the cultures have a vast diversity in terms of the art, architecture, the customs, and manifestations of their human intellect. For example, in many cases, customs and social events like wedding ceremonies may be more closer to non-Muslim fellows in their regions rather than Muslims in other parts of the world.

1.7   Islam and Muslims are not Synonymous

As Muslims come from a variety of cultural background, what they do and practice in their daily lives may come from their cultural, ethnic, and social background and are not necessarily part of Islam as a religion. One should be careful to differentiate between culture and religion.

1.8   Civil Rights and Universal Equality

Muslims believe in universal equality, equal rights, and respect for all with no exceptions. In the words of Prophet Muhammed (PBUH):

All mankind is from Adam and Eve, an Arab has no superiority over a non-Arab nor a non-Arab has any superiority over an Arab; also a white has no superiority over a black nor a black has any superiority over a white - except by piety and good action.

These principles are the basis of Islamic jurisprudence, also known as *Fiqh* in Arabic language. One great manifestation of this universal equality is *Hajj* where everyone, irrespective of age, color of skin, or origin is required to wear the same clothes to demonstrate universal equality.

1.9 Beliefs, Practices and Worship

While there are fundamental beliefs or *Articles of Faith*, Islam is a very practical religion. Muslims perform certain actions in their daily life, also known as *Pillars of Islam*. These will be briefly described in later chapters of this book.

The concept of worship in Islam is all about pleasing Allah according to Islamic principles, Quran and guidance of the Prophet Muhammed (PBUH). While the main prescribed methods of worship manifest in *five pillars of Islam*, everything that a person does to please Allah is an act of worship, even smiling to a fellow human being, working to place food on the table, taking care of parents and family and so on, are all considered acts of worship.

1.10 Few Things Explicitly Forbidden in Islam

Other than the prohibition of obvious commonly known bad behavior, there are few things that are explicitly forbidden in Islam which otherwise may be permissible in some other faiths. Some of these are as follows:

- Eating pork and port products
- Taking interest on loans to multiply one's wealth
- Consuming substances that make one intoxicated
- Gambling and betting

1.11 Sources of Religious Knowledge

One of the main emphasis of Islam is to seek useful knowledge, both religious and otherwise. The first word of Quran revealed to Prophet Muhammed (PBUH) translates into "Read" or "Recite". There is a chapter in Quran with name *Pen*.

There are two main sources of religious knowledge in Islam:

- *Quran* is the first and main source of knowledge and provides guiding principles as well as some specifics, although it is not only a book of rules and regulations.

- **Sunnah** of the Prophet Muhammed (PBUH) is the second source. The Sunnah are the traditions of teachings of Prophet Muhammed (PBUH) and includes everything that Prophet Muhammed (PBUH) said or did.

In Islamic Jurisprudence, if a particular matter is not found in the above sources, people are supposed to do their own research according to the guiding principles from Quran and Sunnah and get consensus on the issues of present times.

قُلْ إِنَّمَا أَنَا بَشَرٌ مِثْلُكُمْ يُوحَىٰ إِلَيَّ أَنَّمَا
إِلَهُكُمْ إِلَهٌ وَاحِدٌ فَاسْتَقِيمُوا إِلَيْهِ
وَاسْتَغْفِرُوهُ ۗ وَوَيْلٌ لِلْمُشْرِكِينَ

Say, O [Muhammad], "I am only a man like you to whom it has been revealed that your god is but one God; so take a straight course to Him and seek His forgiveness." And woe to those who associate others with Allah.

Quran: 41:6

2

Muhammed (PBUH) - The Last Prophet

Muhammed (PBUH) is the last of a series of messengers that started with Adam (PBUH). He was born in the year 571-AD, in what is now called Saudi Arabia, in the city of Makkah. He lived in Makkah for approximately 53 years and then migrated to Madinah where he stayed for the last 10 years of his life. He was born an orphan in the tribe of Quraysh, who are descendants of Prophet Abraham and Ismail.

Muslims believe that Prophet Muhammed (PBUH) is a human being like anyone else except that he was given message from Allah. In Allah's words revealed in Quran:

> *Say, O [Muhammad], "I am only a man like you to whom it has been revealed that your god is but one God; so take a straight course to Him and seek His forgiveness." And woe to those who associate others with Allah - Quran - 41:6*

As the Prophet (PBUH) is the messenger of Allah, obedience of the Prophet is an essential part of the Muslim faith. This has been clarified in Quran as:

> *He who obeys the Messenger has obeyed Allah - Quran - 4:80*

The life, actions and words of Muhammed (PBUH) are documented in great detail and are an important source of Muslim Jurisprudence. This chapter is a very brief introduction for beginners.

7

2.1   Early Life

Abdullah, the father of Prophet Muhammed (PBUH), passed away few months before his birth. His mother also passed away when he was young. He was raised first by his grandfather and then his uncle. He was considered a noble, honest and trustworthy man in Makkah. He started his career as merchant. At the age of 25, he married Khadijah (mother of believers) and had four daughters and two sons with her.

2.2   Quran Revelation in Makkah

The first verses of Quran were revealed to Prophet Muhammed (PBUH) when he was approximately 40 years old. A translation of these verses is as follows:

> *Recite in the name of your Lord who created -*
> *Created man from a clinging substance.*
> *Recite, and your Lord is the most Generous -*
> *Who taught by the pen -*
> *Taught man that which he knew not.*
> Quran 96:1-5

He began preaching to the people of Makkah and continued doing so for the next thirteen years. He faced severe opposition from his tribe. People who accepted Islam in Makkah were persecuted and many migrated to Ethiopia while others faced severe hardships, torture, and a social boycott.

Prophet Muhammed (PBUH) continued receiving revelation of the Quran through angel Gabriel in Makkah. This part of Quran appeals to intellect of people making them think about their pagan beliefs, oneness of God and that there is a life after death where people will be held accountable for what they did in this life.

2.3   The Hijrah - Migration to Madinah

After thirteen years of continuous preaching and struggle, the Prophet (PBUH) migrated to Madinah, a city approximately 300 miles north of Makkah, with other Muslims on the invitation of people of Madinah. This is a big event in Muslim history and marks the beginning of the *Hijri* calendar. The Hijri calendar is also known as the *Muslim Calendar* and is based upon lunar months.

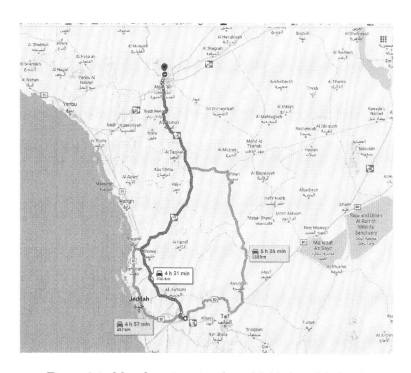

Figure 2.1: Map for migration from Makkah to Madinah

2.4   Life in Madinah

Prophet Muhammed's (PBUH) life in Madinah was full of struggle and under continuous attacks from Makkans. He signed a peace treaty with Makkans in the sixth year after Hijrah, which was later broken by them. After the treaty was broken, he went back to Makkah and conquered the city without a fight, granting immunity to its residents, forgiving everyone who wronged him. He went back to Makkah one last time for Hajj (pilgrimage) in the last year of his life and gave his last major sermon to the Muslims outlining the guiding principles and summarizing his struggle. He passed away soon after that and is buried in Madinah.

2.5   The Last Sermon

The last Hajj sermon outlines the core principles and his priorities for Muslims. The prophet Muhammed (PBUH) praised and glorified Allah in the beginning and then addressed people. The exact wording of the speech are in many books of tradition and narrated by a number of people, but here is a summary:

- O people, listen to my words. I do not know whether I shall ever meet you again in this place after this year.

- O people, your blood and your property are sacrosanct until you meet your Lord, just as this day and this month of yours are sacred.

- Surely you will meet your Lord and He will question you about your deeds.

- Let he who has a pledge return it to the one who entrusted him with it.

- Behold! Everything pertaining to the Days of Ignorance is under my feet and completely abolished.

- Abolished are also the blood-revenges of the Days of Ignorance. The first claim of ours on blood-revenge which I abolish is that of the son of Rabi'a b. al-Harith, who was nursed among the tribe of Sa'd and killed by Hudhail[1].

- And the usury of the pre-Islamic period is abolished, and the first of our usury I abolish is that of 'Abbas b. 'Abd al-Muttalib, for it is all abolished[2].

- Fear Allah concerning women! You have rights over your women and your women have rights over you.

---

[1]Rabi'a was a person of his own tribe
[2]Abbas was his uncle

- O People, no prophet or apostle will come after me, and no new faith will be born. Reason well, therefore, O people, and understand words which I convey to you. I leave behind me two things, the Quran and my example, the Sunnah, and if you follow these you will never go astray.

- All mankind is from Adam and Eve. An Arab has no superiority over a non-Arab, nor does a non-Arab have any superiority over an Arab; a white has no superiority over a black, nor does a black have any superiority over a white; except by piety and good action.

- Know for certain that every Muslim is a brother of another Muslim, and that all Muslims are brethren. It is not lawful for a person [to take] from his brother except that which he has given him willingly, so do not wrong yourselves.

- And you would be asked about me (on the Day of Resurrection), (now tell me) what would you say?

Then he asked people whether he has conveyed the message to them and they replied yes. The he said "O God, bear witness".

2.6 Collection of Hadith and Sunnah

Hadith is what the Prophet (PBUH) said and *Sunnah* is what he did. People have gone to great lengths to document the life of Prophet, what he said, how he acted in different situations, or what he did. An accompanying vast knowledge base is about the lives of people who narrated anything from the Prophet to ensure the narrators themselves are trustworthy both in remembering things and in their character.

2.7 Why Muslims Don't Draw Pictures of Prophet (PBUH)

In the days of ignorance before Prophet Muhammed (PBUH), people used to make images of prophets and other nobles to worship them. Islam categorically prohibits worship of any person or entity except the one and only God. For that reason Muslims have avoided any depiction of a prophet or other noble people. In the current period, Muslims avoid this to show their deep respect for the Prophet (PBUH) and not make it a trivial routine as other religions have done.

2.8   Chapter Summary

Prophet Muhammed (PBUH) was born in Makkah, spent about fifty three (53) years of his life there. Due to continuous persecution he migrated to Madinah and spent last ten years of his life there. Life of Prophet Muhammed (PBUH), as an ordinary person and as a ruler of a state, is the best example for Muslims. His actions and teachings, compiled in the form of *Hadith* books, are the best explanation of Quran, and source of religious knowledge. He is buried next to the grand Mosque of Madinah.

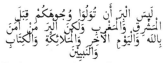

Righteousness is not that you turn your faces toward the east or the west, but [true] righteousness is [in] one who believes in Allah, the Last Day, the angels, the Book, and the prophets. - Quran 2:177

3

Fundamental Beliefs in Islam

There are six major beliefs in Islam as mentioned in Quran and the Hadith. These are also known as *Articles of Faith*. These include oneness of God, belief in existence of angels, prophets, books, life after death and day of judgment, and divine decree. These are briefly described in this chapter.

3.1 Oneness of God

Muslims believe in one and only God, creator and sustainer of this universe. **Allah** is the common Arabic name for the God but Quran has used many other beautiful names as well, commonly known as ninety nine names of Allah. Allah has no physical manifestation, gender, children, spouse, and is absolutely unique. Allah is Almighty and All-Knowing. When Allah decides something to happen, it happens.

> *Say (O Muhammed), He is Allah, the One and Unique, the Self-Sufficient to whom eventually all take their needs. He begets not, nor was He begotten. And none is comparable to Him.* - Quran - 112

Oneness of God is the very basic and fundamental belief to Islam and there is no exception. Muslims also believe that:

- Allah is the only one who should be worshiped.

- People have direct relationship with Allah and need no intermediary.

- Allah is all-knowing, even knowing what one thinks.

- Allah has many attributes described by different names in Quran (e.g. The Most Merciful, The Creator, The King, The Kind, The Great, The Wise)[12].

- Nothing in this universe happens without Allah's knowledge.

- Allah's knowledge supersedes time and space, the seen and the unseen.

- Allah has shown people the right path and the wrong path and given them free will to choose whichever they decide to.

Oneness of God is a fundamental Muslim belief without which a person can't be a Muslim.

3.2   Angels

Angels are created from light, perform different functions with absolute obedience to God, and have no free will. Many angels are mentioned in Quran.

The names of prominent angels mentioned in the Quran and Islamic tradition are the following:

- Jibril (Gabriel) had the responsibility to bring Allah's message to His prophets.

- Mikail (Michael) delivers sustenance and related matters.

- Israfil (Raphael) is assigned to blow the trumpet that will signal end of time and start of the day of judgment.

- Azrael or *Mulk-o-Mout* is the angel of death responsible for taking the soul away.

3.3   Scriptures

A basic Islamic belief is in the books that were given to prophets of Allah. The Quran was revealed to Prophet Muhammed (PBUH) over a period of twenty three years and is the message for all of humanity and not only for Muslims. Other main books that Muslims believe in are:

- Gospels that were given to Prophet Jesus (Isa)

- Torah that was given to Prophet Moses (Musa)

- Psalms given to Prophet David (Dawood)

- Scrolls given to Prophet Abraham (Ibrahim)

These books are mentioned in Quran at different places by name:

> *And We caused Jesus, son of Mary, to follow in their footsteps, confirming that which was (revealed) before him in the Torah, and We bestowed on him the Gospel wherein is guidance and a light, confirming that which was (revealed) before it in the Torah - a guidance and an admonition unto those who ward off (evil). - Quran 5:46*

Muslims believe in divine revelations of these scriptures but believe that the Quran is the only one of them that is preserved in its original form.

3.4 Prophets

Allah has sent prophets to every nation and their message was the same. Twenty five prophets are mentioned in Quran by name including Abraham (Ibrahim), Noah (Nooh), Jonah (Yunus), Moses (Musa), Jesus (Isa), Jacob (Yaqoob), David (Dawood), Joseph (Yusuf) and others. Peace be upon all of them.

> *And for every nation is a messenger. So when their messenger comes, it will be judged between them in justice, and they will not be wronged - Quran 10:47*

Many chapters (Surah) in Quran start with names of prophets. Muslims often name their children after them and believe that all of them conveyed God's message to their nations. Muhammed (PBUH) is the last prophet and messenger from Allah and he was sent to all of humankind and his message is universal.

3.5 The Day of Judgment

Islam provides the principle of accountability for one's actions, which is a necessary and logical consequence of free-will. People who perform good deeds will get their reward in the form of paradise and people with bad deeds will be punished with hell. All people from the beginning to the end of time will be resurrected and will be shown their *book* of deeds.

> *That Day, the people will depart separated [into categories] to be shown [the result of] their deeds.*
> *So whoever does an atom's weight of good will see it,*
> *And whoever does an atom's weight of evil will see it.*
> (Quran - 99:6-8)

This concept of reward and punishment is fundamental to the Muslim belief system. Even the best justice system in this world can't fully punish people who have committed crimes against humanity, or reward people who have spent their lives serving others. There has to be some accountability more than what we have here. Nobody should get away with their extreme bad deeds and nobody should get less reward than what they deserve.

When will the day of judgment happen? This is the question that people used to ask Prophet Muhammed (PBUH) quite often. The Quran answers this questions in many places that only Allah knows about it. When ordered by Allah, angel Israfil will blow the trumpet that will trigger the end of time and start of the day of judgment.

> And they say, "When is this promise, if you should be truthful?"
> Say, "The knowledge is only with Allah, and I am only a clear warner."
> Quran - 67:25:26

3.6   Divine Decree

Muslims believe in the freedom of action and resulting accountability of one's actions on the day of judgment. At the same time they also believe in divine decree involving many things that are not in ones control. For example, place where I was born or when I was born, who are my parents, when will I die, and so on. Other examples include circumstances of my life and whether my actions will be fruitful as I wish because of factors that are not in my control, or natural disasters that change the course of events. For these reasons, one is responsible for intention and actions and not of the results.

Even the prophets are only responsible for making an effort and conveying the message, not whether anyone takes the message and gets guidance.

3.7   Chapter Summary

Articles of Faith described in this chapter are the fundamental beliefs for Muslims. Belief in oneness of God is the centerpiece without which nobody can become a Muslim. Allah has the ultimate knowledge of the past, the present, and the future. Prophets are people who are assigned by Allah to deliver His *message* and *guidance* to the humankind. This guidance was sent in the form of books through His prophets. Muhammed (PBUH) is the last prophet and Quran is the last book of guidance from Allah and supersedes all previous books. Muslims believe that angels are created from light and are assigned to carry out different tasks to run this universe and in the hereafter with Allah's permission. Muslims believe in accountability of their action on the *day of judgment* when all human beings will be resurrected and asked about their deeds in this life.

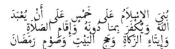

بُنِيَ الإِسْلَامُ عَلَى خَمْسٍ عَلَى أَنْ يُعْبَدَ
اللَّهَ وَيُكْفَرَ بِمَا دُونَهُ وَإِقَامِ الصَّلَاةِ
وَإِيتَاءِ الزَّكَاةِ وَحَجِّ الْبَيْتِ وَصَوْمِ رَمَضَانَ

*(The superstructure of) al-Islam is
raised on five (pillars), i. e. Allah
(alone) should be worshipped, and
(all other gods) beside Him should
be (categorically) denied. Establishment of prayer, the payment
of Zakat, Pilgrimage to the House,
and the fast of Ramadan - Hadith,
Sahih Muslim - 16*

The Five Pillars of Islam

Although Quran does not use word *Pillars of Islam* specifically, there are five fundamental practices that all Muslims perform as their testimony to following Islam as their religion. These practices are all about putting faith into action and make it part of daily life. These are:

1. Testimony or proclamation of faith, also known as *Shahadah*.

2. Five daily prayers or *Salah*.

3. Fasting in the month of Ramadan or *Saum*.

4. Giving a minimum amount of money to charity or *Zakat* on annual basis

5. Performing pilgrimage to Makkah and the House of Allah (Kaaba), also known as *Hajj*, for those who can afford and have means to do so

These five items require Muslims to not only perform rituals but also engage in activities that require their time, effort and money in obedience of Allah and in the care of their fellow human beings.

The following excerpt from Quran covers some of the articles of faith and pillars. There are many places in Quran where these are mentioned in different contexts.

> *Righteousness is not that you turn your faces toward the east or the west,
> but [true] righteousness is [in] one who believes in Allah, the Last Day, the
> angels, the Book, and the prophets and gives wealth, in spite of love for*

> *it, to relatives, orphans, the needy, the traveler, those who ask [for help],*
> *and for freeing slaves; [and who] establishes prayer and gives zakah; [those*
> *who] fulfill their promise when they promise; and [those who] are patient*
> *in poverty and hardship and during battle. Those are the ones who have*
> *been true, and it is those who are the righteous.* - Quran 2:177

These five basics are also mentioned in a number of books of *Hadith* [1]. Some examples are below:

(The superstructure of) al-Islam is raised on five (pillars), i.e. Allah (alone)
should be worshipped, and (all other gods) beside Him should be (categori-
cally) denied. Establishment of prayer, the payment of Zakat, Pilgrimage to
the House, and the fast of Ramadan - Sahih Muslim 16

4.1 Testimony of Faith - *Shahada*

Proclamation or testimony of faith is key to becoming Muslim. Basically it is about making a statement in Arabic that translates to the following:

I bear witness that there is no deity worth worshiping but Allah and Muhammed
(PBUH) is his servant.

Typically when one decides to become a Muslim, he/she will say these words in front of others. While Muslims carry out activities every day, like five daily prayers, just uttering these words is enough to *become* a Muslim.

4.2 Five Daily Prayers - *Salah*

While the afternoon prayer on Friday is the main weekly gathering, Muslims are to pray five times every day. These prayers are key to having a constant contact with Allah and a reminder that everyone has to stand in front of Allah on the day of judgment and be accountable for their deeds.

Prayer Timings

Prayers are done at fixed time (not arbitrarily) every day. Following are the times for Muslim prayers:

1. The morning prayer (*Fajar*) is after dawn and before sunrise.

2. The noon prayer (*Duhur*) is right after past the noon time.

3. The afternoon prayer (*Asr*) is close to middle time between noon and sunset.

---

[1] A *Hadith* is the saying or actions of Prophet Muhammed (PBUH) as documented in books of tradition

4. The evening prayer (*Maghreb*) is performed right after the sunset time.

5. The night prayer (*Isha*) is approximately one hour after the sunset.

The Friday prayer and sermon

The Friday prayer is performed a little after the noon time and is a special weekly prayer for Muslims to come together in each community, meet each other, and listen to sermon from their Imam[2]. This prayer is a replacement in lieu of the second prayer of the day and is known as *Jumua'ah* prayer.

Where to Pray?

While it is preferred to pray in a mosque (Masjid), Muslims are allowed to pray at home or wherever they are at the time of the prayer, as long as it is neat and clean. In essence, all of the earth is considered a Masjid for the purpose of prayer.

What People Say in Prayer?

The opening chapter of Quran (*Al-Fatihah*) is the essential part and is recited in every prayer in Arabic. Its translation is as shown below.

> *In the name of Allah, the Merciful, the Compassionate*
> *Praise be to Allah, the Lord of the entire universe.*
> *The Merciful, the Compassionate*
> *The Master of the Day of Judgment*
> *You alone do we worship, and You alone do we turn for help*
> *Direct us on to the Straight Way*
> *The way of those whom You have favored, who did not incur Your wrath,*
> *who are not astray*

Most Muslims memorize parts of Quran that they recite in the daily prayers after this initial chapter.

Prayer is a physical task

Muslim prayer is a physical practice where they stand up facing Ka'aba in Makkah. There are three main positions during each prayer: Standing, Bowing, and Prostrating.

4.3 Fasting in Ramadan

Muslims fast for one month each year during the month of Ramadan, the ninth month of the lunar calendar. Since the lunar calendar is ten days shorter than Gregorian calendar, Ramadan starts ten days earlier each year.

---

[2]Imam is the leader of community who also leads a prayer in mosque

The purpose of fasting is to seek closeness to Allah by exercising self-restraint and willingly stop doing things that are not forbidden otherwise. For some it is an annual exercise to take a step back, focus on the purpose of their life, do acts of charity and focus on good deeds.

> *O you who have believed, decreed upon you is fasting as it was decreed upon those before you that you may become righteous* - Quran 2:183

Following are few important things to understand about fasting and the month of Ramadan:

- Ramadan is either 29 or 30 days long depending upon lunar cycle. Sighting of a new moon marks the beginning of Ramadan.

- The fasting starts at dawn time and ends at sunset each day. There is no eating, drinking, or smoking during this time. Spousal relationships are also forbidden while one is fasting.

- People usually wake up early morning and eat before dawn. This is called *Suhoor*.

- There is usually a big meal at breaking of fast (sunset time). This meal is called *Iftar* or *Iftari*.

- There is extra prayer after *Isha* prayer at night called *Taraveeh*. It is a tradition to revise Quran from start to end during these prayers.

- All adults are supposed to fast except people who are sick, traveling, old who can't fast, women who are pregnant or nursing, people who have to take medicine for any medical conditions, etc. Basically, the objective of fasting is not to cause harm to anyone.

- People who can't fast because they are old or have permanent medical conditions (like diabetic), are supposed to feed a poor person for each day of not fasting (if they can afford it).

- People who have non-permanent conditions (like traveling) can fast later on (after Ramadan) to make up for days they have not fasted in Ramadan.

- *Eid* is one of the big Muslim festivals that marks the end of Ramadan.

Fasting has been part of other Abrahamic religions as well in some shape or form.

4.4   Zakat - The Charity

Zakat (or Zakah) means purification in Arabic. While followers of Islam are encouraged to offer optional charity and distribute their wealth among those who are less fortunate, Zakat is an obligatory form of charity on those who have savings more than a certain limit. With some exceptions, Muslims are instructed to give away 2.5% of accumulated wealth (or net worth) each year for purposes such as helping the poor, freeing prisoners, slaves and captives, helping travelers who are stranded in foreign lands, helping people pay their debt who can't pay otherwise, and other defined purposes.

Few important aspects of Zakat are:

- Zakat is taken from rich and given to poor and others as described earlier.

- Zakat is an important worship to show submission to Allah from the perspective of money and the acknowledgement that a person performs charity from the wealth that Allah has given him/her in the first place.

- It is an important act to keep money in circulation and avoid accumulation of wealth in few hands.

- While paying Zakat, one should consider needy people who are closest, starting with one's own family and friends.

4.5   Hajj - The Pilgrimage

Hajj or pilgrimage to Makkah and the House of Allah, the *Kaaba*, is performed on specific days during the last month of Islamic lunar calendar. Hajj is obligatory upon all Muslims, once in a lifetime, if they can afford to and have the means to do so. Many save money throughout their life to be able to go to Hajj, especially those who live far away from Makkah.

Why Hajj?

Hajj is *the* epic act of worship and a spiritual journey for Muslims. It combines acts of worship that include physical effort, monetary expenditure, and travel. It is a kind of an annual world-wide assembly of Muslims where they walk on the footsteps of prophets and practically demonstrate the principles of equality of all human beings by wearing same type of clothes and performing the same rituals together, without any differentiation of the color of their skin or socioeconomic status.

What is Kaaba?

Kaaba is an almost cube shaped structure in the center of grand mosque Makkah, in Saudia Arabia. It is the *"House of Allah"* and all Muslims face towards Kaaba for prayers.

> *Indeed, the first House [of worship] established for mankind was that at Makkah - blessed and a guidance for the worlds. In it [Kaaba] are clear signs [such as] the standing place of Abraham. And whoever enters it shall*

> be safe. And [due] to Allah from the people is a pilgrimage to the House -
> for whoever is able to find thereto a way. But whoever disbelieves - then
> indeed, Allah is free from need of the worlds. - Quran 3:96-97

The Rituals

A typical Hajj is four to five days long. It is a sequence of rituals that starts on
day 8th of the Islamic month of Dilhajj and continues till Day 13. In summary,
Hajj is not complete until a person [3]:

- Dresses in two plain and unstitched white pieces of clothes (*Ihram*) to
  acknowledge and demonstrate equality of all humankind irrespective of
  nationality, color of skin, social status, language or anything that divides
  people[4]. Hajj is a manifestation of unity and equality.

- Attends the main sermon of Hajj in plain of Arafat which is about 12
  miles outside of Makkah.

- Circumambulates the Kaaba seven times to remind oneself that the *center* of his/her whole life is the obedience of Allah.

- Walks on the footsteps of a woman (Hajra or Hager) from the mount of
  Safa to the mount of *Marva* to commemorate her search for water for
  her baby son, Ismail. Walks normally where she walked normally and
  runs where she ran.

- Sacrifices an animal to commemorate Prophet Ibrahim's obedience to
  Allah in his willingness to sacrifice his son.

- Throw stones at three pillars that are a symbolic representation of Satan
  for three days to reject Satan's way and commemorate the actions of
  Prophet Ibrahim.

The main event of Hajj is 9th day of Dilhajj (the twelfth month of Islamic
Calendar) when all people get together in the plain of Arafat (an open land
outside Makkah) and the Hajj sermon is delivered.

Malcolm X's Experience of Hajj

Hajj is a spiritual journey and many people have written about their experience
throughout the history. Malcolm X (El Hajj Malik El Shabazz) is a prominent
figure in civil right movement in the United States. He went for Hajj in 1964
which changed his perspective about racism and equality and he wrote the
following letter from Makkah [6]:

Never have I witnessed such sincere hospitality and overwhelming spirit of true
brotherhood as is practiced by people of all colors and races here in this ancient
Holy Land, the home of Abraham, Muhammad and all the other Prophets of

---

[3]This is only a summary of activities

[4]This is necessary only for men. Women can wear their normal clothes.

the Holy Scriptures. For the past week, I have been utterly speechless and spellbound by the graciousness I see displayed all around me by people of all colors.

I have been blessed to visit the Holy City of Mecca, I have made my seven circuits around the Ka'ba, led by a young Mutawaf named Muhammad, I drank water from the well of the Zam Zam[5]. I ran seven times back and forth between the hills of Mt. Al-Safa and Al Marwah[6]. I have prayed in the ancient city of Mina, and I have prayed on Mt. Arafat.

There were tens of thousands of pilgrims, from all over the world. They were of all colors, from blue-eyed blondes to black-skinned Africans. But we were all participating in the same ritual, displaying a spirit of unity and brotherhood that my experiences in America had led me to believe never could exist between the white and non-white.

America needs to understand Islam, because this is the one religion that erases from its society the race problem. Throughout my travels in the Muslim world, I have met, talked to, and even eaten with people who in America would have been considered white - but the white attitude was removed from their minds by the religion of Islam. I have never before seen sincere and true brotherhood practiced by all colors together, irrespective of their color.

You may be shocked by these words coming from me. But on this pilgrimage, what I have seen, and experienced, has forced me to rearrange much of my thought-patterns previously held, and to toss aside some of my previous conclusions. This was not too difficult for me. Despite my firm convictions, I have always been a man who tries to face facts, and to accept the reality of life as new experience and new knowledge unfolds it. I have always kept an open mind, which is necessary to the flexibility that must go hand in hand with every form of intelligent search for truth.

During the past eleven days here in the Muslim world, I have eaten from the same plate, drunk from the same glass, and slept on the same rug - while praying to the same God - with fellow Muslims, whose eyes were the bluest of blue, whose hair was the blondest of blond, and whose skin was the whitest of white. And in the words and in the deeds of the white Muslims, I felt the same sincerity that I felt among the black African Muslims of Nigeria, Sudan and Ghana.

We were truly all the same (brothers) - because their belief in one God had removed the white from their minds, the white from their behavior, and the white from their attitude.

I could see from this, that perhaps if white Americans could accept the Oneness of God, then perhaps, too, they could accept in reality the Oneness of

---

[5]Zam Zam is a fountain of water under the Grand Mosque in Makkah

[6]Two mountains in Makkah, close to Ka'ba

Man - and cease to measure, and hinder, and harm others in terms of their 'differences' in color.

With racism plaguing America like an incurable cancer, the so-called 'Christian' white American heart should be more receptive to a proven solution to such a destructive problem. Perhaps it could be in time to save America from imminent disaster - the same destruction brought upon Germany by racism that eventually destroyed the Germans themselves.

Each hour here in the Holy Land enables me to have greater spiritual insights into what is happening in America between black and white. The American Negro never can be blamed for his racial animosities - he is only reacting to four hundred years of the conscious racism of the American whites. But as racism leads America up the suicide path, I do believe, from the experiences that I have had with them, that the whites of the younger generation, in the colleges and universities, will see the handwriting on the walls and many of them will turn to the spiritual path of truth - the only way left to America to ward off the disaster that racism inevitably must lead to.

Never have I been so highly honored. Never have I been made to feel more humble and unworthy. Who would believe the blessings that have been heaped upon an American Negro? A few nights ago, a man who would be called in America a white man, a United Nations diplomat, an ambassador, a companion of kings, gave me his hotel suite, his bed.

. . .

Never would I have even thought of dreaming that I would ever be a recipient of such honors - honors that in America would be bestowed upon a King - not a Negro.

All praise is due to Allah, the Lord of all the Worlds.

Sincerely,

El-Hajj Malik El-Shabazz (Malcolm X)[6]

4.6 Chapter Summary

Islam is a very practical religion. It demands action from its followers in daily life to demonstrate their belief and have a continuous connection with their creator. These actions require allocating time for daily prayers, an *annual refresher course* in the form of fasting in Ramadan, walking on the footsteps of prophets to perform *Hajj*, and purifying their wealth through *Zakat*. From a practical perspective, these practices ensure that Muslims demonstrate their belief in equality of all human beings through standing together in their daily prayers and performing Hajj rituals. Practice of charity through Zakat provide a means such that wealth is continuously redistributed in society.

أَفَلَا يَتَدَبَّرُونَ الْقُرْآنَ أَمْ عَلَىٰ قُلُوبٍ أَقْفَالُهَا

Will they not contemplate the Quran? Do they have locks on their hearts?

47:24

5

Quran: The Most Recited Book

The Quran (aka Koran) is the religious text of Islam revealed to Prophet Muhammed by Allah over a period of approximately twenty-three years through angel Gabriel. Muslims believe this to be the final revelation from Allah to humankind that supersedes previous divine books like the Torah and the Bible. The Quran is in Arabic and is perfectly preserved in its original form down to each word and letter. No matter which part of the world you go, you will find exactly the same version of Quran in its original form in the Arabic language. How it has been preserved will be discussed shortly[5].

The Quran is divided into 114 chapters, each called a *Surah*. Some are as small as few lines while others much are larger. Each *Surah* consists of verses called an *Ayah*. Muslims recite the Quran in their daily prayers and memorize at least some part of it. The first Surah (Al-Fatihah) is recited in each prayer. Memorizing the whole Quran is a continuous tradition from the days of Prophet Muhammed (PBUH). It is also a tradition to recite the entire Quran during the special night prayers in the month of Ramadan.

The word *Quran* literally means a book that is recited and is mentioned many times in the Quran itself. Without any doubt this is the most recited book every day around the globe, hence the name is the most appropriate one. The name also reflects the first word that was revealed to Prophet Muhammed *"Read"* or *"Recite"*. Allah has used many other names for the book in different parts of the Quran to show that this book provides guidance, is a light, is a differentiator, a reminder, and so on.

5.1   Revelation of Quran

As mentioned earlier, the Quran was revealed to Prophet Muhammed (PBUH) over a period of twenty-three years starting when he was 40 years of age. The first revelation of Quran consists of five verses and emphasizes on reading and knowledge. A translation of these verses is shown below.

> *Recite in the name of your Lord who created -*
> *Created man from a clinging substance.*
> *Recite, and your Lord is the most Generous -*
> *Who taught by the pen -*
> *Taught man that which he knew not.*
> *(Quran 96:1-5)*

The initial chapters of Quran revealed in Makkah are called *Makki Surahs.* They emphasize on faith, arguments about oneness of God, and that there is a life after death where people will be held accountable for their deeds. These are more poetic in nature. The later chapters that were revealed after the HIjrah (migration to Madinah) cover more lengthy topics related to a Muslim society and are called *Madani Surahs.* Each chapter is named by picking a word or a topic discussed in the chapter.

5.2   Al-Fatihah - The First Chapter of Quran

The opening chapter of Quran consists of seven verses and is named *Fatihah* which in Arabic means "the opening" or beginning. Translation of this chapter is shown below.

> *In the name of Allah, the Merciful, the Compassionate*
> *Praise be to Allah, the Lord of the entire universe.*
> *The Merciful, the Compassionate*
> *The Master of the Day of Judgment*
> *You alone do we worship, and You alone do we turn for help*
> *Direct us on to the Straight Way*
> *The way of those whom You have favored, who did not incur Your wrath,*
> *who are not astray*

This is one of the most important parts of Quran and is recited in each of the five daily prayers. Some have said that this is a prayer from a person to Allah requesting for guidance and that the rest of the Quran is the answer to their prayer.

5.3 Style of Quran

Most people who read the Quran are initially surprised because it is not like any other ordinary book with organized chapters and topics. It is more like a speech to humankind from Allah. The Quran makes arguments and uses different methods to make a point. Sometimes it uses anecdotes and stories of previous nations. At other times it appeals to the intellect of people that this universe was not created in vain, rather, there is a purpose. In some chapters it asks question after question to make people think.

The Quran has addressed not only Muslims but the entire human race. It is a book of intellect and does not ask people to have a blind faith in Allah.

The Quran has many stories about previous nations but it is not a story book. It refers to historical events to make a point without going into detail of these stories.

The Quran is a unique book and one of its own kind. New readers of Quran should take it like that to fully understand it.

5.4 Tradition of Recitation and Memorization

Since the initial days of Quranic revelation, it has been a tradition for Muslims to memorize Quran and recite it in daily prayers. Most Muslims have memorized some part of Quran and there are many who memorize all of it. People who memorize the whole Quran are commonly known as *Hafiz* which in Arabic translates to *protector*.

The leader of daily prayers or *Imam* in each Masjid recites the opening chapter, *the Fatihah*, followed by some other parts of Quran. It is a tradition that if the Imam makes a mistake while reciting, someone will correct the Imam on the spot. There is no exception to it. Even if the Imam of the Grand Mosque in Makkah makes a slight mistake in recitation, he will be corrected right at that moment. Other than the written form of Quran, this is one of the reason it is not possible for anyone to make even a slight change to the text. As described in Quran itself, Allah has taken the responsibility of protecting it.

> *Indeed, it is We who sent down the Quran and indeed, We will be its guardian* Quran - 15:9

Since the Quran is the last revelation from Allah, it is logical that its authenticity has to be beyond any doubt. Memorization and daily recitation is one means for its protection but it is a separate topic in itself.

5.4.1   Recitation in Month of Ramadan

Ramadan is the ninth month of Muslim calendar. Muslims practice fasting in this month, which is a pillar of Islam. Muslims offer additional prayers called *Taraweeh* during this month and there is a tradition to recite the entire Quran during Taraweeh. This provides an opportunity for people to listen to the whole book and for reciters to refresh their memorization.

5.5   Quranic Calligraphy

Over centuries, many Muslims have translated their love of Quran into calligraphic art. There are many writing styles and fonts adopted by artists in different part of the world. Figure 5.1 is an eleventh century writing in *Kufic* style[1].

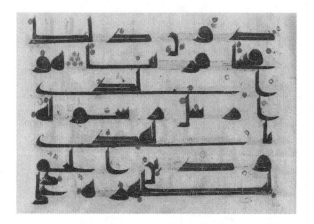

Figure 5.1: Quran in Kufic Script - 11th century

5.6   Emphasis on Learning

As mentioned earlier, the Quran puts a great emphasis on knowledge and learning. It asks people to ponder on the universe around them and how it is created and sustained. It encourages exploring the creation around oneself, gain knowledge and find signs of its creator. It tells people that humans are the best creation of Allah and given the intellect to understand the universe.

---

[1] https://en.wikipedia.org/wiki/Kufic#/media/File:Qur%27an_folio_11th_century_kufic.jpg

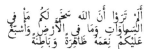

Do you not see that Allah has
made subject to you whatever is in
the heavens and whatever is in the
earth and amply bestowed upon
you His favors, [both] apparent and
unapparent?

Quran: 31:20

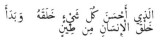

Who perfected everything which
He created and began the creation
of man from clay.

Quran: 32:7

Fine Arts and Culture

While the contributions of Muslims in advancement of fine arts, architecture,
and culture is well-known, this chapter provides just a sample of Islam's view
on bringing out the best of people in these fields, starting with a saying from
Prophet Muhammed (PBUH) describing beauty.

Allah is Beautiful and Loves Beauty

*Prophet (PBUH) said, "No one will enter Paradise who has an atom's
weight of pride in his heart." A man said, "What if a man likes his
clothes to look good and his shoes to look good?" He said, "Allah is
beautiful and loves beauty. Pride means denying the truth and looking
down on people." [Related by Muslim 131]*

Contributions of Muslim civilization to humanity are numerous to count in a
short text like this. "Muslim Heritage"[4] is a good online resource understand
some of these contributions towards culture and society of today.

6.1 Calligraphy

In the initial periods, Muslims did not draw human pictures to avoid the
pitfall of falling back into worshiping personalities and idols. They focused
their artistic efforts on Calligraphy and other forms of art. However, in the

later periods when that danger faded away, drawings of humans and other living creatures became a common place in books of science and art.

Figures 6.1, 6.2 and 6.3 are some samples of Quranic calligraphy from older times [9] [10]. This tradition continues till today and most iconic buildings in Muslim majority countries have calligraphy as an essential part of their interior decoration. Figure 6.3 is a photograph taken at Cleveland Museum of Arts [7].

Figure 6.1: Smithsonian - Folio from a Koran, Sura 5, verses 12-13, 13th century, Maghribi Script

Figure 6.2: Quran in Early Kufic Script - 9th century

6.2   Patterns and Tile Work

Muslim architects have been building beautiful patterns for centuries with geometrical shapes. People have written books on these patterns and courses are offered in universities about this form of art. Figure 6.4 shows some amazing

Figure 6.3: Calligraphy - Credits Cleveland Museum of Arts

patterns and tile-work which is a hallmark of many buildings in the Central Asian region [14].

Figure 6.4: A beautiful architecture from Samarkand, Central Asia

6.3 Architecture

While there are many masterpieces of architecture built by Muslim architects and engineers, Taj Mahal [13] in India, Masjid Wazir Khan in Pakistan, Sheikh Zaid Masjid in Abu Dhabi, King Faisal Mosque in Islamabad are just few examples.

Figure 6.5: Taj Mahal in Agra, India build by Mughal Empror Shah Jahan

Figure 6.6: Sheikh Zayed Masjid in Abu Dhabi

6.4 Vase and Household Items

Artifacts made of china, brass, and other materials are commonplace for art work on household items. Some pieces of art are shown in Figures 6.7, 6.8 and 6.9.

Persian carpets are very famous all over the world for their fine finishing and patterns.

Figure 6.7: A metal bowl, Source - Cleveland Museum of Arts

Figure 6.8: Fine art work on metal, Source - Cleveland Museum of Arts

Figure 6.9: A jar with calligraphy, Source - Cleveland Museum of Arts

بِسْمِ اللهِ الرَّحْمَنِ الرَّحِيمِ
In the name of Allah, the most
beneficient, the most merciful

Start of Quran

7

Myths about Islam

While Islamophobia is one of the primary reasons for a number of myths about Islam and Muslims, diversity of cultures and encroachment of extraneous norms into Muslim societies have created some confusion as well. Muslims are not at the high levels of morals as Islam wants them to be. Some people unfairly generalize the bad acts of few to the entire Muslim societies and to Islam. This chapter briefly describes some of these myths.

7.1   Gender Equality and Relationships

Both women and men have very important roles in society with opportunities to utilize their potential. Khadijah, wife of Prophet Muhammed (PBUH) was a wealthy woman and had her own trade business. The Quran mentions the Queen of Sheba who was a sovereign ruler (Quran, Chapter 27). While women are not treated justly in some cultures and some parts of the world, it is very unfair to attach these issues to Islam.

7.1.1   Equality

Women and men enjoy equal rights and equal accountability over their lives such as owning property, doing businesses, choosing their spouses, and in other parts of life.

> *Allah has promised the believing men and believing women gardens beneath which rivers flow, wherein they abide eternally* - Quran - 9:72
>
> *And their Lord responded to them, "Never will I allow to be lost the work of [any] worker among you, whether male or female; you are of one another.* Quran - 3:195

Both women and men are expected to dress modestly and uphold social and moral norms and values.

Women and men also play their roles in the family structure where they are equal but not the same in the responsibilities. Men are responsible for providing for their family, women are not required to share family's financial burden and they can keep their earning as they play a bigger role in raising their children. Anybody who studies the Muslim family system based purely on Islam will come to the conclusion that it is the most fair and just arrangement between a woman and a man.

7.1.2   Women Share in Inheritance

Both women and men are given their fair share in inheritance.

> *For men is a share of what the parents and close relatives leave, and for women is a share of what the parents and close relatives leave, be it little or much - an obligatory share.* Quran - 4:7

Share for different stakeholders are defined in Quran according to their responsibilities. While on the face of it, there may appear to be a disparity, when reviewed in the context of expectations, they are very equitable, if not favorable for women.

7.1.3   Prominent Contemporary Muslim Women in Political Leadership Roles

What is common about these Muslim women? They are or have been at the highest political position of a country, either a president or a prime minister[11].

- Diah Permata Megawati Setiawati Sukarnoputri - President of Indonesia from 2001 to 2004

- Benazir Bhutto, a Pakistani politician who twice served as Prime Minister of Pakistan; first from 1988 to 1990 and again from 1993 to 1996

- Mame Madior Boye served as Prime Minister of Senegal from 2001 to 2002

- Bibi Ameenah Firdaus Gurib-Fakim is a Mauritian politician and served as the President of Mauritius from 2015 to 2018

- Sheikh Hasina Wajid is the Prime Minister of Bangladesh since January 2009, the longest serving prime minister in the history of Bangladesh

- Halimah Yacob current president of Singapore

7.2 Muslims are Arabs

While Prophet Muhammed (PBUH) was an Arab, many people think of Muslims and Arabs as synonyms. This could not be farther from reality. Arabs are actually a minority of the overall Muslim population across the globe. Figure 7.1 shows distributions of Muslim population in different regions as published by the Pew Research Center.

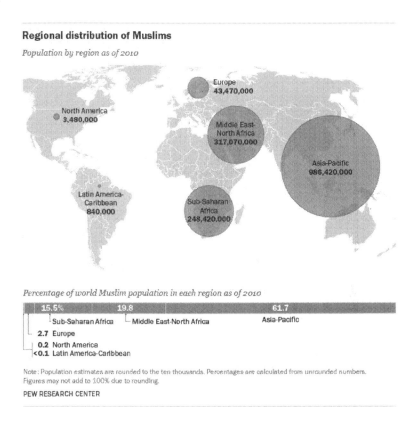

Figure 7.1: Pew Research map for Muslim population in different regions as of 2010

According to Pew Research Center[2], top five countries with highest Muslim population are as follows. As you can see Egypt is the only country from the Middle East region.

1. Indonesia

2. Pakistan

3. India

4. Bangladesh

5. Egypt

Asians are the largest part of Muslim population, the Middle East and North Africa combined comes second followed by sub-Saharan Africa. Europe and United States have small Muslim population.

7.3 All Muslims Speak Arabic Language

Although Quran is in Arabic but a vast majority of Muslims actually doesn't speak or understand Arabic language. Muslims are spread all over the globe and speak different languages like Urdu, Farsi, Bengali, Malay, Swahili, English, and others. However, most of the Muslims use some Arabic words in their daily conversation. For example:

- *In Sha Allah* - God Willing

- *Ma Sha Allah* - An expression for seeing or listening of something good

- *Assalam-o-Alaikum* - Peace be upon you, a standard Muslim greeting

7.4 Muslim Contributions to Humanity

It is very clear the history curriculum in many schools need to be updated as they jump from Greek philosophers to Renaissance period, omitting many centuries of great work done by Muslim scientists, engineers, philosophers, architects, doctors, and artists. The National Geographic published an article about how early Islamic Science advanced medicine[1]. There are many other texts describing contributions of *House of Wisdom* established by Caliph Haroon ul-Rahid, Al-Razi (Rhazes), Al-Zahrawi (Abulcasis), the *Canon of Medicine* written by Ibn Sina (Avicenna) which is a five volume book on medicine, and many others.

7.4.1 Prominent Contemporary Muslims

Following are some prominent names well-recognized globally for their contributions in different fields.

- **Muhammed Ali** - The greatest boxer of all times, the champion of the people

- **Malcolm-X** - Prominent leader of civil rights movement

- **Kareem Abdul Jabbar** - Professional NBA basketball player for the Milwaukee Bucks and the Los Angeles Lakers

- **Muhammed Yunus** - Nobel Peach Prize winner known for his work in poverty alleviation through micro financing

- **Malalah Yusufzai** - Nobel Peace Prize winner known for championing girls education

- **Cat Stevens / Yusuf Islam** - A famous British singer-song writer who converted to Islam and changed his name from Cat Stevens to Yusuf Islam

7.4.2   Literature and Poetry

Anyone with an interest in literature and poetry knows the work or Rumi, Hafiz, Omar Khayyam and many others. The names are numerous and beyond the scope of this short book but a quick search on the Internet will be helpful for those who are interested.

Appendix A: Free Quran Resources

Following are few sources for getting a copy of Quran:

Online

An authentic online source of Quran is at https://quran.com where you can find many translations of Quran along with the Arabic text. This web site also provides you search capability for research purposes.

Print

You can request printed copy of Quran from *Send a Quran*, a project of Al-Furqan Foundation - https://sendaquran.com/

Furqan Project is another related resource to request a copy of Quran at https://furqaanproject.org

Bibliography

[1] Víctor Pallejà de Bustinza. *How Early Islamic Science Advanced Medicine.* 2016. URL: https://www.nationalgeographic.com/archaeology-and-history/magazine/2016/11-12/muslim-medicine-scientific-discovery-islam/.

[2] Pew Research Center. *Interactive Data Table: World Muslim Population by Country.* 2017. URL: https://www.pewforum.org/chart/interactive-data-table-world-muslim-population-by-country/.

[3] Creative Commons. *Creative Common Licenses.* 2017. URL: https://creativecommons.org/licenses/.

[4] Technology Foundation for Science and Civilization. *Muslim Heritage: Discover the Golden Age of Muslim Civilization.* 2019. URL: http://www.muslimheritage.com/.

[5] Why Islam. *Quran: A Miracle to last till the End.* 2014. URL: https://www.whyislam.org/islam/the-preservation/.

[6] *The Autobiography of Malcolm X: As Told to Alex Haley.* Ballantine Books, 1987.

[7] *The Cleveland Museum of Arts.* 2019. URL: http://www.clevelandart.org/.

[8] Wikipedia. *Allah Logo without background.* URL: https://commons.wikimedia.org/wiki/File:Allah_logo.svg.

[9] Wikipedia. *Folio of Quran, Surah 5, verses 12-13 from Koran in Maghribi Script from Smithsonian, United States public comain.* URL: https://commons.wikimedia.org/wiki/File:Maghribi_script_sura_5.jpg.

[10] Wikipedia. *Kufic script, 8th or 9th century (Surah 48: 27-28).* URL: https://en.wikipedia.org/wiki/Kufic#/media/File:Folio_from_a_Koran_(8th-9th_century).jpg.

[11] Wikipedia. *Muslim women political leaders.* 2019. URL: https://en.wikipedia.org/wiki/Muslim_women_political_leaders.

[12] Wikipedia. *Names of Allah.* URL: https://simple.wikipedia.org/wiki/Names_of_God_in_Islam.

[13] Wikipedia. *Tah Mahal in city of Agra, India.* URL: https://en.wikipedia.org/wiki/Taj_Mahal#/media/File:Taj_Mahal_inside_view_02.JPG.

[14] Wikipedia. *Ulughbek Madrasa in Samarkand.* URL: https://en.wikipedia.org/wiki/Samarkand#/media/File:Samarkand,_Registan,_Ulugbek_Medressa_(6238565020).jpg.

[15] Wikipedia. *World Muslim Population by Percentage.* URL: https://upload.wikimedia.org/wikipedia/commons/2/21/World_Muslim_Population_Map.png.